HOLLAND LOP RABBIT MANNUAL

A DETAILED GUIDE ON HOW TO CARE, FEED, TRAIN, GROOM, HEALTH, HOUSE HOLLAND LOP RABBITS AND GUIDELINES TO RAISING THEM AS PETS

ANN HARPER

Made with ♥ on the Notion Press Platform
www.notionpress.com

Contents

Title Page

HOLLAND LOP RABBIT MANNUAL

A detailed guide on how to care, feed, train, groom, health, house Holland lop rabbits and guidelines to raising them as pets

Ann Harper

CHAPTER ONE

INTRODUCTION TO THE CARE OF HOLLAND LOP RABBITS

Holland Lop rabbits are the tiniest lop-eared rabbits. This endearing miniature rabbit breed developed in

It originated in the Netherlands and has grown to be an immensely popular pet worldwide.

Adults typically weigh between 2-4 pounds and have a sociable, lively, and sweet demeanor, making them great pets for families with young children or for those who live in tiny quarters.

Enter Caption

HISTORY AND ORIGIN OF HOLLAND LOP RABBITS

Adrian de Cock was the first to breed Holland Lops in the Netherlands.

He desired a bigger version of the Dutch Dwarf rabbit with French Lop ears.

He was eventually successful, thanks to some breed strengthening from an English Lop.

In 1964, the Netherlands Governing Rabbit Council recognized the Holland Lop, followed by the American Rabbit Breeders Association in 1979.

They were bred expressly as pets, and as a result, they are not only adorable, but also gentle and simple to care for.

CHARACTERISTICS OF THE HOLLAND LOP RABBIT

Enter Caption

SIZE

The Holland Lop is a dwarf rabbit, thus they are only around 4-5 inches tall, and 10-12 inches long when stretched. They may reach a weight of four pounds.

BODY

Holland Lops have compact bodies that are surprisingly robust for their size, measuring around the same width as they are tall.

The ratio of body to head is around 2:1. Their noses are small and rounded, and their ears are long and almond-shaped.

COAT AND COLOR

Holland Lops come in a variety of colors and patterns and have short to medium-length silky fur.

TEMPERAMENT

Holland Lops are quite active for their size and enjoy a variety of activities.

They thrive on attention and are often pleasant and sociable.

Additionally, they are considered to be quite curious, which might get them in hot water.

Many people prefer the lively, sociable, inquisitive, and sweet Holland Lop over more docile, cuddly types.

LIFESPAN

Holland Lops have a lifespan of around 5-7 years.

CHAPTER TWO

EVERYTHING ABOUT HOLLAND LOP RABBIT

CARING FOR THEM

Enter Caption

Holland Lop rabbits are regarded for being quite simple to care for, which is another reason for their popularity as pets.

They are immune to genetic ailments and have readily maintained coats and claws.

If you are already experienced with rabbit care, they will be a piece of cake.

The following are some of the most important aspects of Holland Lop rabbit care:

COAT

Although Holland Lops have short hair that does not tangle readily, they nevertheless need coat upkeep.

As with cats, rabbits should be brushed often to minimize the quantity of hair consumed when grooming.

Brush your Holland Lop at least once a week and more often during the shedding season.

Brushing is also an excellent opportunity to evaluate your Holland Lop, examining their teeth, feet, and overall health.

CLAWS

Indoor-only rabbits are often at danger of developing enlarged claws, which may become unpleasant.

Nails should be cut and examined every month or two.

TEETH

As with the nails, if a rabbit's diet is overly soft, its teeth may become too long.

Providing enough of hay and good chewing toys aids in teeth prevention.

EXERCISE

Holland Lops need a high level of activity and exercise. Assure them that their house is spacious and filled with exciting and intriguing toys.

If they reside inside, try installing a rabbit run outside to let them to run free for an hour or two each day.

HEALTH

Holland Lop rabbits are prone to ordinary rabbit ailments, and should be regularly monitored for changes in feeding or drinking habits, as well as behavioral changes.

It's always a good idea to examine their coats, body, teeth, and paws on a monthly basis.

At the very least once a year, all rabbits should be examined by a veterinarian.

SPAY/NEUTER

Prior to purchasing a Holland Lop, it's usually a good idea to locate a veterinarian in your area who is experienced with rabbits.

Not all veterinarians are experienced with smaller animals, and anesthetizing a very small rabbit for dental care or spaying might be challenging.

Spaying or neutering your rabbit may help avoid some health problems and provide them with a more balanced temperament, but it's important to contact a reputable veterinarian and explore your choices.

FEEDING

All rabbits need an endless supply of fresh, clean water.

Certain Holland Lop rabbits may have digestive troubles, and most rabbits thrive on a diet that is balanced and constant, rather than one that is varied.

Choose a very high-quality pellet with a low protein content, a high fiber content, and a balanced vitamin and mineral content.

Examine the contents list on your rabbit pellets to ensure they are of good quality and natural origin.

Following pellets, use a high-quality hay.

Rabbits need hay in their meals to maintain a healthy digestive tract, and timothy hay is excellent for a Holland Lop's teeth.

If their pellets already include alfalfa hay, do not supplement with extra alfalfa hay.

You may sometimes feed treats to adult Holland Lops, but not to adolescents.

COST OF THE HOLLAND LOP

A pet-quality Holland Lop normally costs between $25 and $50 when purchased from a reputable breeder. Holland Lops of show quality might cost much more.

CHAPTER THREE

Holland Lop Rabbit Care

Holland Lop rabbits, with their small stature and floppy ears, are the embodiment of cuteness. They are a little breed of rabbit that matures to reach between three and four pounds. If you learn how to properly care for your Holland Lop rabbit, it will live a happy and healthy life in your house.

Making a Rabbit's Home

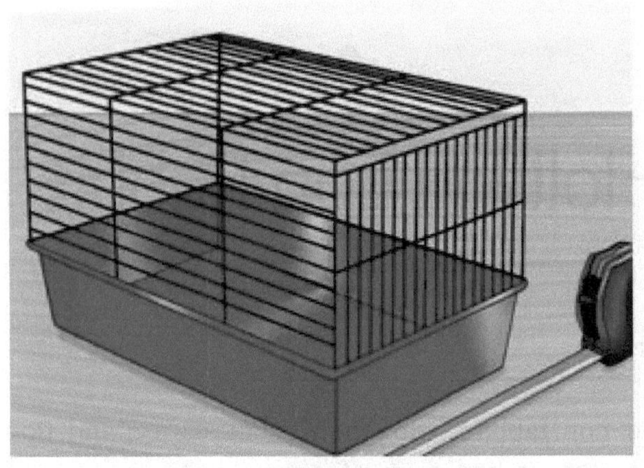

Enter Caption

1. Construct a rabbit cage. You'll want to prepare a cage for your Holland Lop rabbit prior to bringing it home. Choose a cage that is at least one square foot in size for each pound of fully grown rabbit. That is at least a four-foot square cage for a Holland Lop rabbit. They are quite active, so ensure that your rabbit has lots of space to run. The width of the cage should be 1.5 times the length of the fully grown rabbit, while the length of the cage should be three times the bunny's length. For instance, a rabbit measuring 12 inches (30.5 cm) in length should have a width of 18 inches (45.7 cm) and a length of 36 inches (91.4 cm). That is the rabbit's exclusive space.

• You'll also require room in the cage for a litter box with litter, her food and drink bowls, and a box for her to relax, so aim for at least double that amount of floor area.

2. Purchase a cage that has a sturdy/solid floor.

Ensure that the cage has a solid floor rather than a wire floor. Wire flooring may create sores on your rabbit's feet, and tiny rabbits such as the Holland Lop can get trapped and hurt. Along the bottom of the cage, place a piece of carpeting or hardwood flooring.

• Alternatively, you may use a piece of fleece cloth, since it will not leave lengthy strings in the rabbit's digestive track if it eats it.

• Newspaper may also be used to line the cage; however, newspaper should not be used as bedding.

• Bear in mind that you will also need to cover the floor with bedding to offer padding for the rabbit.

3. Furnish the cage with bedding.

Enter Caption

Even if the floor is firm, the cage requires bedding. The bedding will serve as a sleeping space for your rabbit. The bedding should be edible, since it will be consumed by your rabbit. Meadow or timothy hay, natural fiber blankets, pelleted paper, or other organic bedding materials all make excellent bedding.

• Allow her enough space to shape, move, and burrow in it as she pleases.

• Check and clean the bedding everyday. If your rabbit is going to the toilet in the bedding, you must provide a greater space for the rabbit to wander, exercise, and move about. Fleas, flies, and other pests may breed in unclean bedding.

• Avoid bedding materials such as straw, cardboard, newspaper, wood shavings, sawdust, cat litter, or cedar or pine products. It may cause injury to your rabbit.

4. Decide whether you want to keep your rabbit cage inside or outside.

Both habitats have their merits. Indoor rabbits often live longer, are happier, and are more sociable. Rabbits that live outside are fearful and vulnerable to temperature and weather fluctuations, predators, mites, flies, and fleas, among other dangers.

• If you want to keep your rabbit inside but have limited area for her to move about and play, you may build up an outdoor cage for her.

• Outdoor hutches are simpler to maintain and provide more space for the rabbit to run and play. If you choose to play your hutch outdoors, keep it away from direct sunlight, drafts, damp areas, extreme temperatures, or loud noises. The hutch should have a roof to keep her dry during inclement weather. Assure that the hutch is safe from predators like as dogs and cats.

5. Provide a litter box for your pet.

Enter Caption

Insert a box inside the cage of your rabbit to serve as a litter box. A medium-sized plastic cat litter pan will enough for a little Holland lop rabbit. It is preferable to get a larger litter box than a smaller one. Place new hay inside the litter box. Additionally, you may add bunny-safe pet bedding underneath the hay.

• Create a box with a kitchen end and a bathroom end. They will use the bathroom end to relieve themselves, while the kitchen end will be used to graze on clean hay.

• If you have more than one rabbit, either a big litter box or separate boxes for each bunny.

• Frequently change your bunny's hay to keep it clean. Bunnies will utilize a clean litter box but will avoid one that is filthy. Do not leave the litter box alone for more than two days. To clean, just toss everything into the trash, replace the bedding with fresh bunny-safe material, and wash the box.

• You should confine him to this cage until he begins using the litter box regularly.

6. Establish a place for hiding.

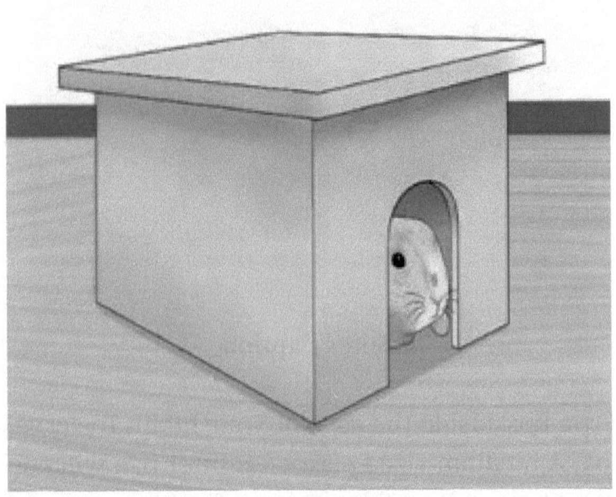

Enter Caption

Rabbits are inherently fearful and prefer to conceal themselves from predators, loud sounds, and other things that frighten them. You must offer suitable hiding areas for your rabbits, such as a cardboard box, a series of cardboard tube tunnels, or a low enclosed location that is readily accessible. Additionally, you may buy rabbit hiding spots from a pet shop.

CHAPTER FOUR

Rabbit-Proofing Your Home

1. Consider providing an indoor space for your rabbit.

Enter Caption

If you keep your rabbit inside, you may designate one area for him to run about in. This room should include a designated space for a litter box, hay feeder, food dishes, and water bowl. Protect it from messes by placing a mat underneath it. You may create cardboard castles, bunny condominiums, puppy kennels, or rabbit cages within the space.

2. Electrical wires should be covered or removed.

Rabbits are continually chewing. If you want to let your rabbit run about a room, you must safeguard it by concealing or eliminating wires. Hide and protect electrical lines with a lengthwise split of rigid plastic tubing with the cords tucked within. Additionally, you may disguise cables by tucking them under woodwork or trim, wrapping them in spiral wrap, or using concealers.

Enter Caption

3. Prevent chewing on trim and furniture.

Rabbits will gnaw on trim, door edges, and the legs of furniture. Additionally, they may chew on wallpaper, sheetrock, and carpet. Cover any areas where your rabbit may want to gnaw with a board. Place cardboard or 2x4s under furniture to prevent the rabbit from burrowing into the soft underside. Additionally, clear plastic panels can be placed over the wall to deter the rabbit from chewing on it.

• Keep an eye on your rabbit as she runs about the room and provide her with an appropriate chewing item if she attempts to chew on furniture or other parts of the home.

4. Maintain a plenty of chewable items for your rabbit.

Enter Caption

To help dissuade your rabbit from chewing on things she shouldn't, supply lots of chewable items. Alfalfa cubes, grass hay packed into cardboard tubes, fresh branches (apple, willow, or aspen only), and wrapped up cotton towels are all examples of these.

CHAPTER FIVE

Feeding Your Rabbit

1. A water dish should be placed in the cage.

As a water dish, you may use a sipper bottle or a ceramic dish. While a sipper bottle is more sanitary, rabbits seem to prefer drinking from porcelain plates.

• If you let your rabbit to run about in a room, ensure that she has access to lots of water.

2. Give your rabbit hay.

Enter Caption

Rabbits need the proper quantity of fiber and hydration each day to keep a healthy stomach. Otherwise, they may suffer from illness and may even die. A high-quality grass hay is a staple of a Holland Lop's diet. Grass hay should be supplied indefinitely. Discard any damaged or soggy hay and provide your Holland Lop with new hay every day.

- Grass hay is preferable to alfalfa hay, which is too heavy in protein and calcium to be provided as a food source.

3. Provide pellets for your rabbit.

A commercial rabbit pellet is another mainstay of a rabbit's diet. This is superior to grain or seed mixtures since it is specifically developed for bunnies and has all the nutrients they need. If a rabbit is given a seed or grain mixture, she will choose the components she like and discard the others, resulting in an imbalanced diet.

- An adult Holland Lop rabbit can consume between 18 and 14 cup of pellets per day.
- Ensure that you change the pellets daily to ensure that your rabbit receives fresh pellets.

4. Provide greens for your rabbit.

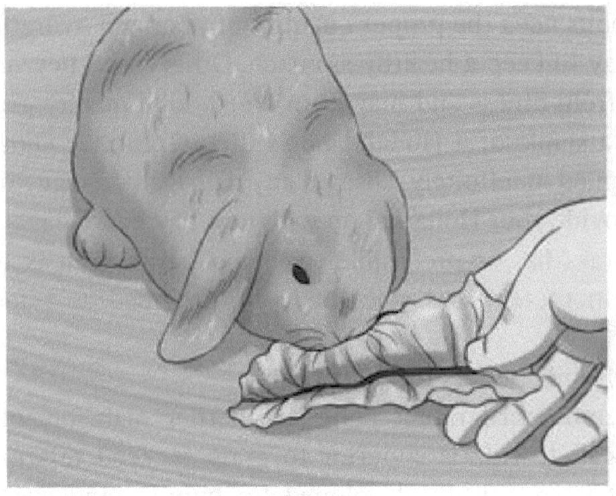

Enter Caption

Green leafy vegetables are necessary for the diet to include fiber and moisture. All types of lettuce, save iceberg, are good options, as are bok choy, broccoli stems and leaves, carrot tops, and dandelion greens. Feed your Holland Lop between 12 and 1 loose cup of these every day.

5. Provide goodies for your rabbit.

Bunnies may consume starchy vegetables such as carrot roots and fresh fruit in moderation, but no more than a few tablespoons each day. Never feed rabbits any other human food, including maize or other grains. Maintain the bulk of the bunny's diet with hay, pellets, and green vegetables.

CHAPTER SIX

Steps to Taking Proper Care Of Your Rabbit

1. Consult a veterinarian about your rabbit.

Many Holland lop rabbits are known to be healthy so long they are fed with the right diet. However, she requires a veterinary check once a year to ensure she is healthy. This inspection will involve a dental examination to ensure that the teeth are adequately worn. If not, the veterinarian may need to clip them to avoid injury to the mouth or teeth.

2. Neuter or spay your rabbit.

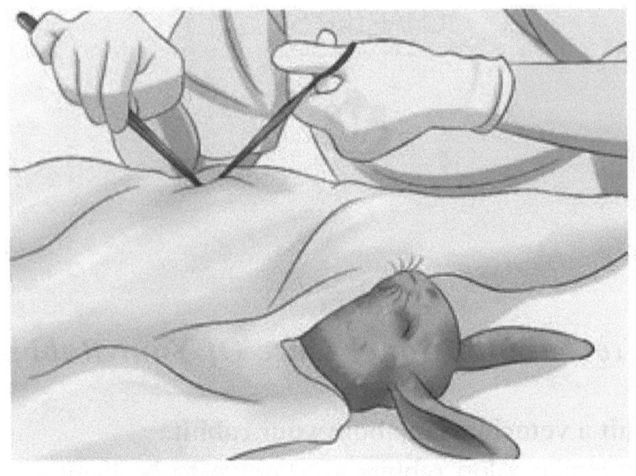

Enter Caption

When your rabbit is 4 to 6 months old, he or she should be neutered if he is a male or spayed if she is a girl. This prevents undesired litters, as well as undesirable behaviors like as hostility or urine spraying, if you have two rabbits of the opposite sex. Additionally, it eradicates tumors and infections of the reproductive system.

3. Keep an eye out for symptoms of disease.

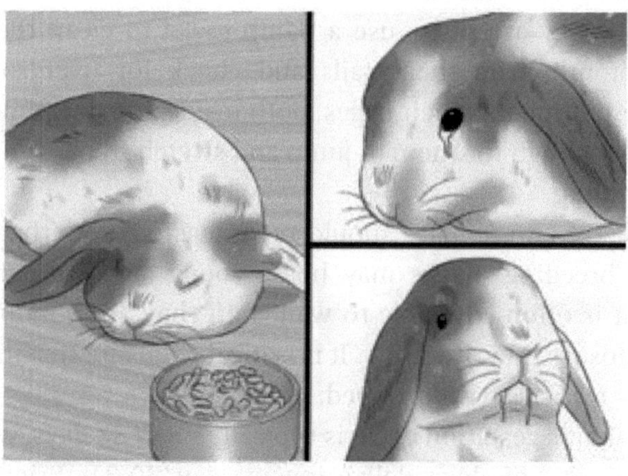

Enter Caption

Rabbits that are fed properly are generally healthy. However, you should be aware of the symptoms of illness, which include refusal to eat or drink, diarrhea, inability to poo for a day, eye or nasal discharge, drooling, swellings, reddened skin, or fur loss anywhere on the body, inability to hop or move normally or inability to use back legs, dark, red urine, or a fever greater than 105 °F (41 °C).

• Never disregard these warning indicators. If you spot them, immediately call your veterinarian for an inspection.

Grooming

Holland Lops require weekly grooming at the very least. You can even do it more frequently during their molting period to avoid wool blocks, which the rabbits may ingest. This is because they typically groom themselves. When fur accumulates, it can obstruct their digestive system.

Bathing your rabbits is not recommended as it stresses them. If they are dirty, use a damp towel to clean them. Each month, trim their nails and check for overgrown teeth. Additionally, their cages, both inside and out, should be large enough for them to jump and stretch freely.

Breeding

Holland Lop females should be at least six months old before breeding. Bucks may be as young as 4.5 months, while it is often advisable to wait until they are 6 months old to ensure they are ready. It is critical to ensure that male rabbits‘ testicles have dropped.

A rabbit's gestation cycle is typically 28 to 33 days, with the majority of does delivering on day 30-31. Prior to breeding, schedule a day for birth so that you may be there to offer the doe with her nesting box. Additionally, it is recommended to plan ahead to ensure that you will be present for the two months during which the babies must remain with their mother, to avoid any complications before they are weaned.

Rabbits are capable of conception and birth at any time of the year. During the warmer summer months, the infants may cause the mother discomfort. Winter births are extremely risky for newborns, since they are born bald. If the mother does not recover, they may all perish. As a result, the optimal seasons for a doe to get pregnant are in the spring and fall.

Clubs and Organizations

With the breed's popularity comes a slew of organizations and groups comprised of Holland Lop enthusiasts. The American Rabbit Breeders' Association (ARBA), the American Fuzzy Lop Rabbit Club, the American Cavy Breeders Association, and the Holland Lop Specialty Club are among these organizations.

CHAPTER SEVEN

FREQUENTLY ASKED QUESTIONS AND ANSWERS

What should the weight of a Holland Lop be?

Holland Lops are approximately three to four pounds in weight. This is the optimal body weight. However, three pounds is the optimal weight for the show ring. These rabbits are widely renowned for their cobby and short bodies, with round heads, and overall enormous look, despite being a little sized rabbit. As an owner, if you discover that your pet's weight is different from the recommended weight, it may be necessary to monitor his or her health.

How are Holland Lop Rabbits used?

At an average of 3.5 pounds, Holland Lops are no doubt acknowledged as the perfect home pets. They vary from other rabbit breeds, such as the American Fuzzy Lop, in that they are non-aggressive as pets. Additionally, they have fur instead of wool. If you're searching for a true dwarf rabbit, Holland Lop rabbits are your best bet. They are small and make excellent household pets.

At what point in their development are Holland Lops considered fully grown?

When dwarf breeds such as the Holland Lops reach the age of six months, they are considered fully grown.

What portion size should Holland Lops consume?

A Holland Lop of average size may swallow 12 cup of pellets per day. They may be administered at any time, but the suggested routine is 14 cup in the morning and another at night. Additionally, they may be given all at once, particularly if you are heading away for the day, or as training rewards throughout the day. This is the suggested diet for them.

Do Holland Lops have an odor?

Unlike other domesticated animals, such as dogs, rabbits have no body odor. This means you will not detect any stench emanating from them. On the other side, if they are suffering from certain illnesses, such as an ear infection, they may emit an unpleasant musty odor. At times, a buck or an entire male rabbit may emit a musky odor, particularly when he is near a female.

Do Holland Lops bite

Occasionally, rabbits may nip in order to attract attention. If you detect this behavior in your pet, some owners advocate shrieking loudly to notify the rabbit. Apart from nipping, they may bite viciously for attention. Additionally, these behaviors occur when they are very hostile or territorial.

Do Holland Lops have a lot of shedding?

Holland Lops, on average, undergo a large and clean molt at least once a year. Following that, they will retain a lovely coat for many months. With this kind of molt, surplus hair may be removed daily by brushing your rabbit to remove as much dead fur as possible. Take note that your rabbit will not get ill throughout this treatment. When wool breed rabbits shred, they appear hideous.

How long do Holland Lops live on average?

Miniature and dwarf rabbits have an average lifespan of roughly 9 to 10 years. In comparison, the bigger breeds of lop eared rabbits have an average lifespan of roughly 5 to 6 years. Holland Lop rabbits typically live between 5 and 7 years. As with other breeds, a lop rabbit may live up to ten years following neutering.

What kind of food do Holland Lop rabbits consume?

Rabbits can eat both starchy vegetables, such as carrot roots, and fresh fruits. They should, however, be fed just a few teaspoons of such food every day. When feeding lops, one thing to keep in mind is that they should not be given human foods like as wheat or maize. It is okay to restrict their diet to pellets, hay, and green vegetables.

Are Holland Lops simple to care for?

Since Lops are little, they are typically simple to manage. In truth, they simply require simple grooming.

How can I determine whether or not my bunny is content?

By and large, rabbits exhibit no visible evidence of emotion, either pleasure or suffering. However, you may observe changes in your bunny's behavior that suggest their pleasure.

Do rabbits cry?

Yes, they do have tear ducts, which cause them to weep. It is, however, distinct from the way people weep. To get a rabbit to weep, great pain or fear must occur, as well as a very saddening emotional experience. They cry in audible tones and noises when they whimper or scream.

Is it feasible to teach a rabbit to behave properly?

There are several techniques available. The first is vocal training. In doing so, anytime your rabbit does anything he or she shouldn't do, call his name and say "NO" in a forceful tone. You can also use the "nose down" technique, which involves gently but firmly pushing your rabbit's nose toward the floor with your index finger while saying his name and the word "no."

Are Holland Lops known to hold grudges?

Rabbits, in general, may harbor a resentment if they are not apologized to. They are capable of sulking for many days. When a rabbit is offended, they will walk away, preferably beyond easy reach. If you find your rabbit entirely withdrawing and tucking its ears behind its back, a major enmity is brewing.

Do rabbits have an excellent memory?

Rabbits have incredible memory. This type of memory is often referred to as orientation memory. This occurs when you spend a lot of time with your rabbits and they develop an attachment to the pattern they always follow when they're around you.

CONCLUSION

Holland Lop rabbits or bunnies are excellent pets. This docile creature is extremely affectionate toward those who look after it.

By providing them with basic necessities such as fresh water and hay, they will easily submit to your attention.

The End

Printed by Libri Plureos GmbH in Hamburg,
Germany